AUGUSTA READ THOMAS

DANCING HELIX RITUALS

FOR VIOLIN, CLARINET, AND PIANO

ED 4617

First Printing: September 2015

ISBN: 978-1-4950-4852-4

G. SCHIRMER, Inc.

DISTRIBUTED BY

HAL•LEONARD®
CORPORATION

7777 W. BLUEMOUND RD. P.O. BOX 13819 MILWAUKEE, WI 53213

halleonard.com

musicsalesclassical.com

Program Note

This 7 minute and 30 second trio was inspired by the generosity, spirit, energy, and dedication of the Verdehr Trio to whom Augusta offers heartfelt gratitude.

Commissioned by the Verdehr Trio and Michigan State University and dedicated with admiration to the Verdehr Trio, "Dancing Helix Rituals" was composed in 2006 and premiered by the Trio on October 21 at the Phillips Collection in Washington, DC. Music reviewer, Stephen Brookes of The Washington Post wrote: *"The standout piece was Augusta Read Thomas's 'Dancing Helix Rituals' from 2006. It's a dance, certainly – but a wild, driving, exhilarating dance that hurtled out of the gate and built into a riot of jazzy rhythms and colorful gestures. Like all good rituals, it was intoxicating — and the trio brought it off with a fine, eloquent frenzy."*

Somewhat of a cross between "Jazz" (Monk, Coltrane, Tatum, Miles Davis, etc.), and "Classical" (Bartok, Stravinsky, Varèse, Berio, Boulez), "Dancing Helix Rituals" can be heard as a lively dance made up of a series of outgrowths and variations, which are organic and, at every level, concerned with transformations and connections. Each player serves as a protagonist as well as fulcrum point on and around which all others' musical force-fields rotate, bloom and proliferate. There is refined logic to every nuance, which stems from the sound, in context, on its own terms. The form is that of a crescendo.

"Dancing Helix Rituals" should be performed in conjunction with dancers when feasible. The early Stravinsky ballets are works Augusta studies, holds in great reverence, loves, and embraces. Augusta sings, dances, moves, and conducts as she composes. As a result, she tends to hear and feel most of her music as music suitable for dance.

The score is marked with words including: *passionate, bright, driving, with flair and ritualistic energy, clock-like and mechanical, scurrying and playful, majestic and stately, funky: romp-like, syncopated, jazzy, colorful, fanfare-like, light* and *bouncy.* Varied, colorful, unexpected musical crosscuts are virtuosically performed in a manner so as to feel spontaneous and yet inevitable.

Duration 7 minutes 30 Seconds

Commissioned by the Verdehr Trio and Michigan State University
Dedicated with admiration to the Verdehr Trio

DANCING HELIX RITUALS
(for Violin, Clarinet, and Piano)
This music should be performed along with dancers when possible.

Augusta Read Thomas
2006

(Transposed Score)

♩ = 100 Passionate, bright, driving, with flair and ritualistic energy★

★All accents should be punchy, especially in the jazzy, syncopated music.

★★All bowing suggestions are optional.

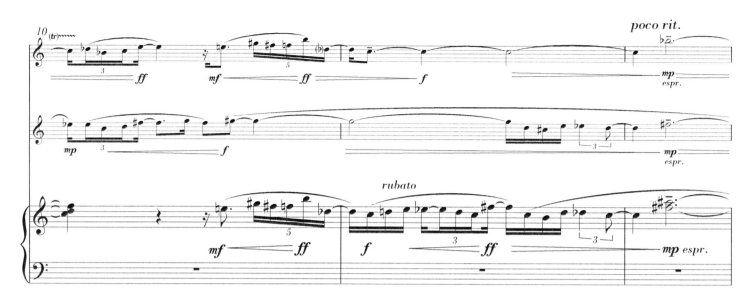

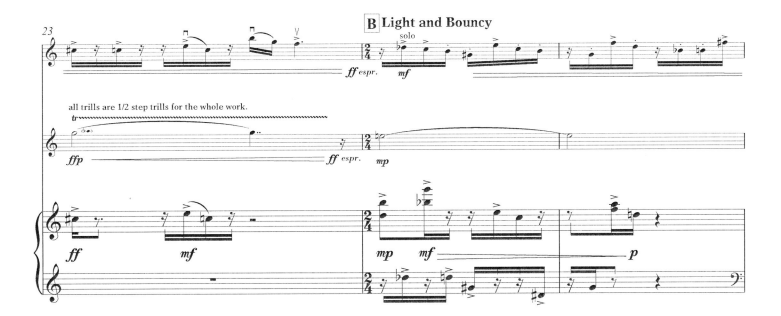

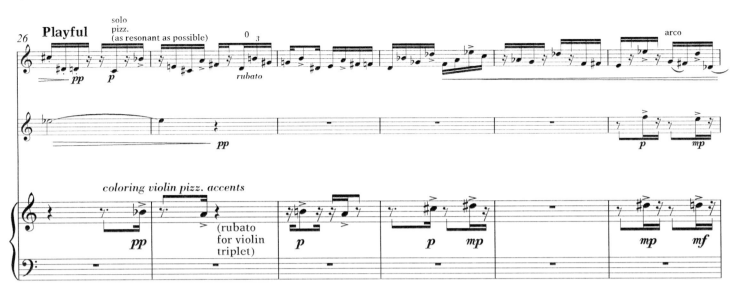

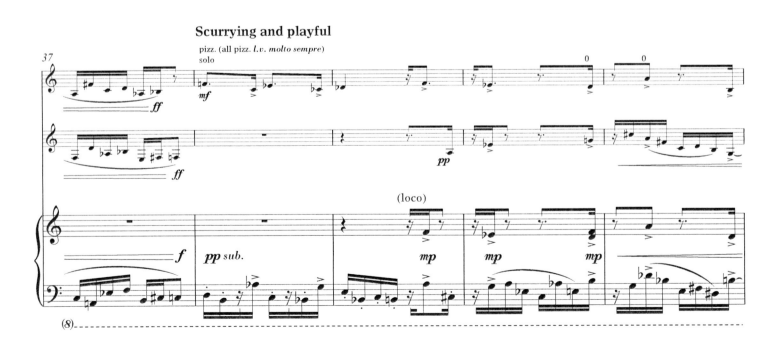

The piano notation shows various voices and phrases of the music.
Clearly color the various voices using hand-crossings and hand-sharings.

D **Bright and spritely; colorful**

pizz (as resonant as possible)

The piano notation shows various voices and phrases of the music.
Clearly color the various voices using hand-crossings and hand-sharings

Passionate and driving

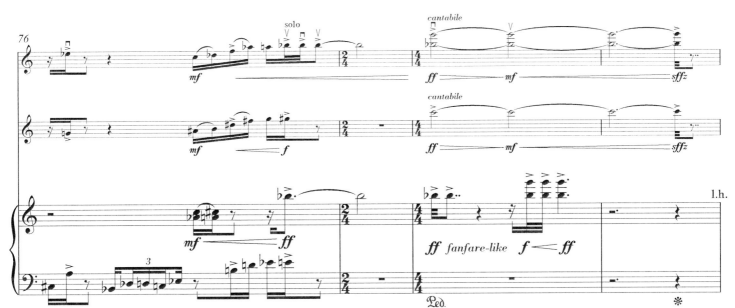

The piano notation shows various voices and phrases of the music.
Clearly color the various voices using hand-crossings and hand-sharings.

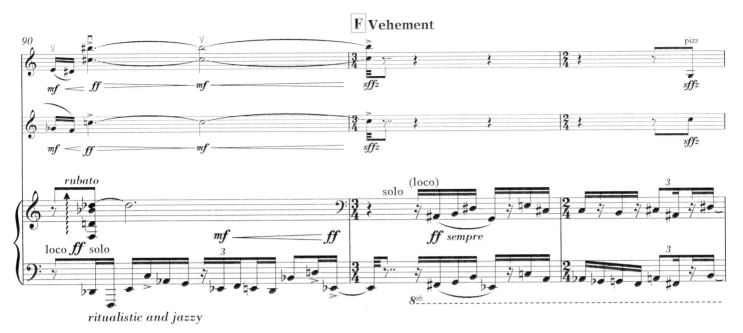

G Fanfare-like

The piano notation shows various voices and phrases of the music.
Clearly color the various voices using hand-crossings and hand-sharings.

all trills are 1/2 step trills for the whole work.

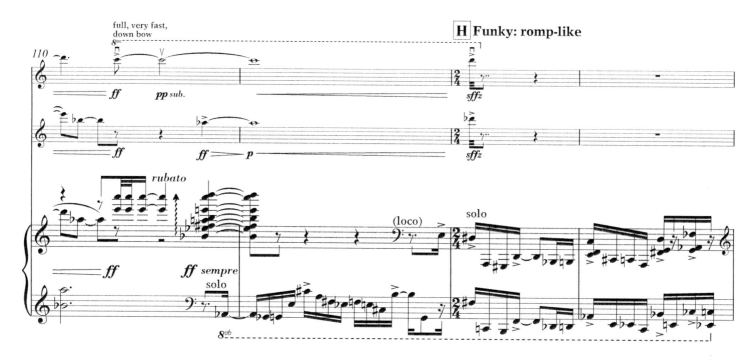

H Funky: romp-like

AUGUSTA READ THOMAS

DANCING HELIX RITUALS

FOR VIOLIN, CLARINET, AND PIANO

VIOLIN

ED 4617
First Printing: September 2015

ISBN: 978-1-4950-4852-4

G. SCHIRMER, Inc.

DISTRIBUTED BY

HAL•LEONARD®
CORPORATION
7777 W. BLUEMOUND RD. P.O. BOX 13819 MILWAUKEE, WI 53213

halleonard.com
musicsalesclassical.com

Violin

Commissioned by the Verdehr Trio and Michigan State University
Dedicated with admiration to the Verdehr Trio

DANCING HELIX RITUALS
(for Violin, Clarinet, and Piano)

Augusta Read Thomas
2006

This music should be performed along with dancers when possible.

*All accents should be punchy, especially in the jazzy, syncopated music.
**All bowing suggestions are optional.

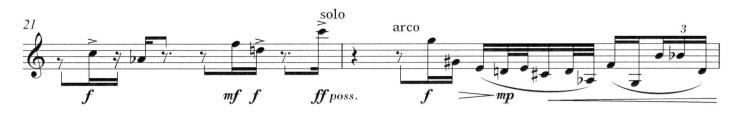

B **Light and Bouncy**

Playful

Scurrying

Scurrying and playful

C **Majestic and stately**

Scurrying and playful

D **Bright and spritely; colorful**

Passionate and driving

F **Vehement**

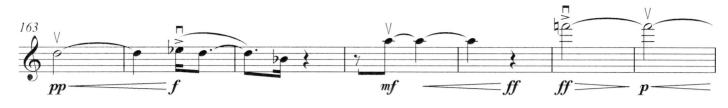

L **Vivid**

M **Dancing Helix**
(all 3 parts swirling at once)

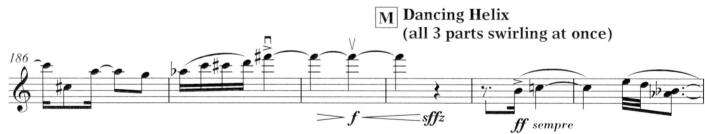

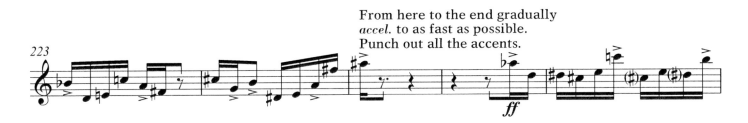

From here to the end gradually
accel. to as fast as possible.
Punch out all the accents.

Duration 7' 30"
Chicago, November 2006

Clarinet in B♭

Commissioned by the Verdehr Trio and Michigan State University
Dedicated with admiration to the Verdehr Trio

DANCING HELIX RITUALS
(for Violin, Clarinet, and Piano)
This music should be performed along with dancers when possible.

Augusta Read Thomas
2006

♩ = 100 Passionate, bright, driving, with flair and ritualistic energy★

all trills are 1/2 step trills
for the whole work.

★All accents should be punchy, especially in the jazzy, syncopated music.

K Cantabile

L Vivid

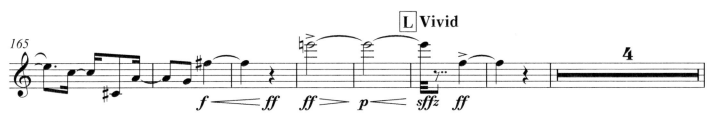

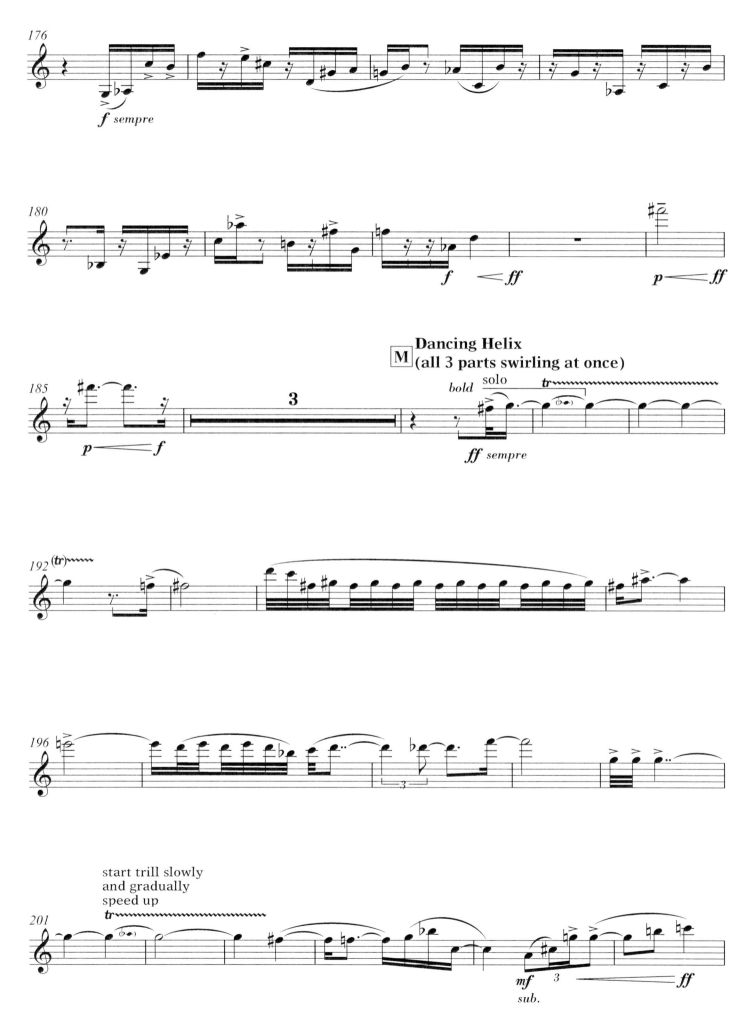

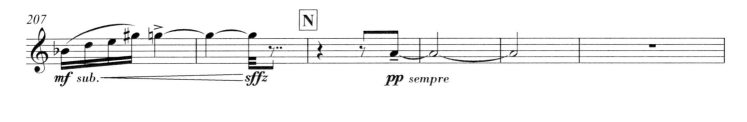

From here to the end gradually
accel. to as fast as possible.
Punch out all the accents.

Duration 7' 30"
Chicago, November 2006

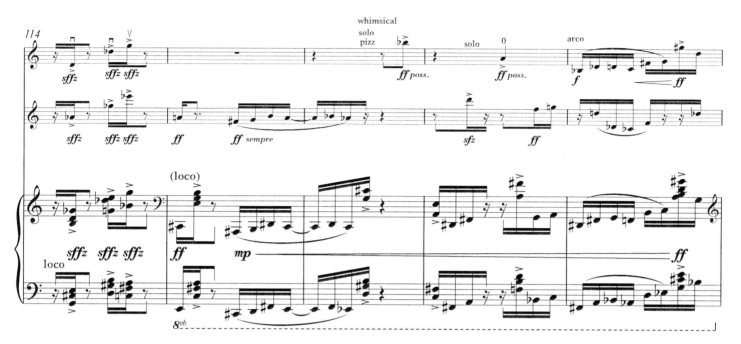

I Lighter and bouncy

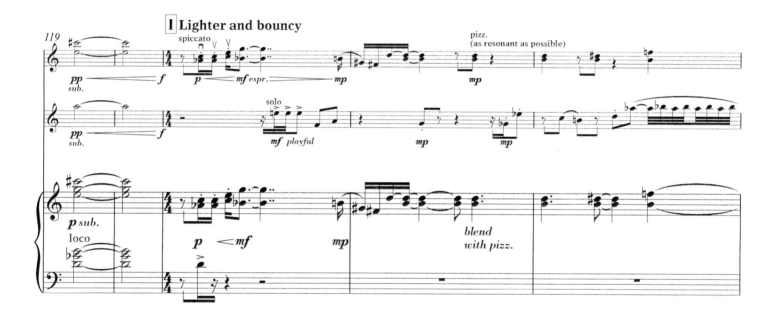

Light and Bouncy

J Mechanical and clock-like

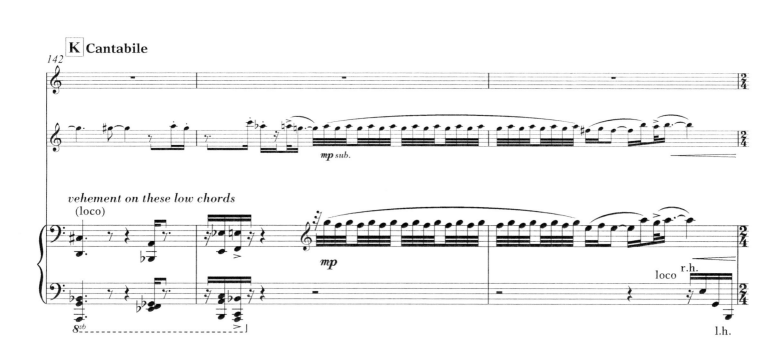

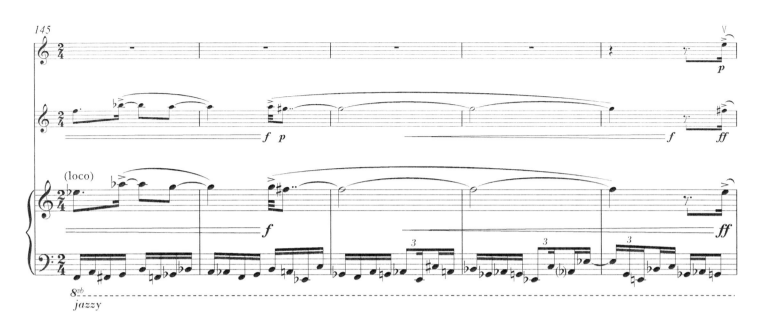

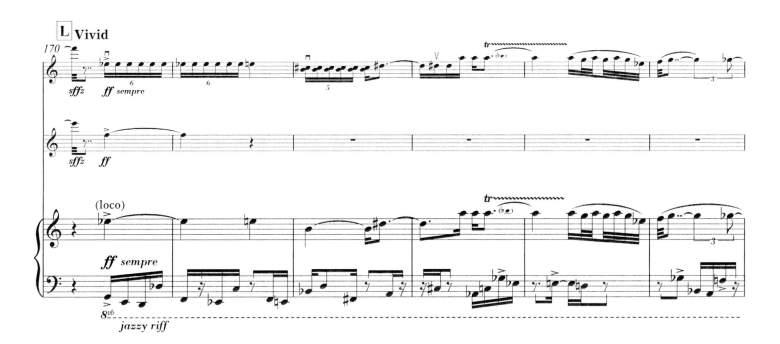

M Dancing Helix
(all 3 parts swirling at once)

From here to the end gradually
accel. to as fast as possible.
Punch out all the accents.

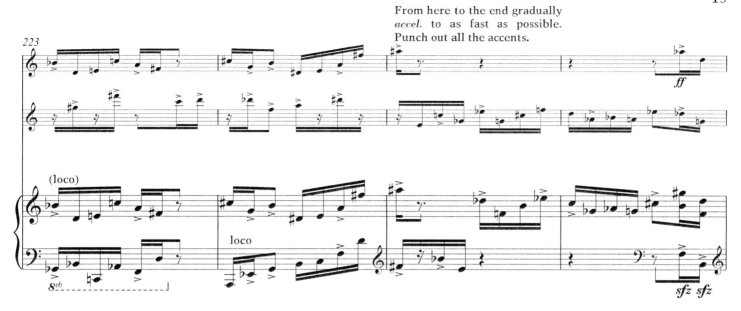

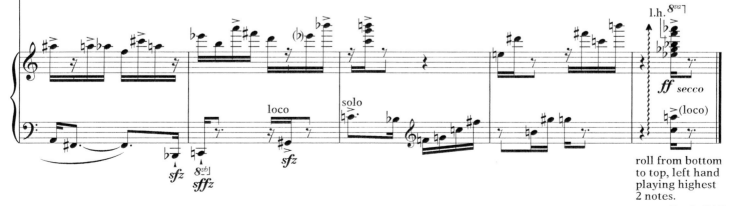

roll from bottom
to top, left hand
playing highest
2 notes.

Duration 7' 30"
Chicago, November 2006